STFU
It's Your Spirit Talkin

How to quiet the noise and listen to
your "Higher Self" when it counts

ADE CRUSE

STFU It's Your Spirit Talkin Copyright © 2019 by Ade Cruse

All rights reserved.

This book may not be reproduced in any form, or by means electronic, mechanical, photocopying, recording, or other, without prior written permission, except by a reviewer who includes brief quotations in a review.

Library of Congress Control Number: 2019902946

ISBN: 978-0-578-47720-6

Interior design by: May Graphics

www.maygraphicspace.com

For my daughter, daddy wrote his first book.

Table of Contents

MY HIGH BREAKTHROUGH 1

WAKING THE DEAD 8

The 20 Secrets Of Spiritual Wealth 18

ideas. 23

ego. 25

attachment. 30

comfort. 32

balance. 34

persistence. 36

projection. 38

adapt. 40

frequency. 43

give. 45

optimism. 48

surrender. 50

action. 52

intention. 54

fear. 57

gratitude. 59

growth. 61

forgiveness 63

"Rule Of P." 68

Purpose 69

Progress. 70

Patience. 71

Leap of Faith Index 73

My High Breakthrough

I'm aware in any minute I won't have your attention for much longer. It's expected. Just finishing this paragraph has been a struggle. I've already changed six diapers, watched several YouTube videos and streamed way too many of my favorite songs on Spotify. That's why for the remainder of this book I promise to cut straight to the fucking point. You could've been binge-watching on Netflix, but you're here with me. I appreciate that.

A few years ago my faith was nonexistent. I gagged at anything remotely esoteric. The part of me that longed for the inner connectivity to self competed with the remaining percentage that didn't care to search for a deeper meaning. It felt like a job that required a lot of work I didn't want to do and time that I didn't have. I was all over the place. My thoughts were scattered, as were my actions.

There was too much outside noise to hear my inner voice. I couldn't even remember my passcode to unlock my phone. A mess. Externally, I was on fire. I had a song on the radio, phone calls from celebrities and cosigned by my favorite music producers. I thought I had everything I wanted. I couldn't explain to myself why I felt so empty. My spirit was suffering from unemployment while my ego had a thriving career with a 401k plan and benefits. The universe just needed one more reason to fire me.

When a touring musician came to my city, I was offered the chance to be an opener for the show. I'll add this act previously had the number one song in the country. This is the kind of opportunity you jump at the chance to be a part of. Every bone in my body told me to accept the offer. Instead, I declined the invitation. What!? You're probably thinking this guy is nuts. You're right! That was the dumbest shit I've ever done. It's every artist dream to have their talent recognized by the masses in some form or another. Nah, not mine. I had my chance, and I blew it! Someone get this guy a schedule for the next karmic lesson.

Shortly after my declaration of stupidity my manager and I parted ways. He went on to sign a talented kid from the area that blew up. When I say blew up I mean this kid was all over TV, red carpets and at every event, Hollywood could throw. It would be dishonest to say I wasn't jealous. I thought I hated him. But, after replaying my decisions over and over again in my mind I realized, I hated myself. Word traveled fast. Everyone thought I was a loser. Any room I was in had six elephants standing around blowing their trunks calling me an idiot. When I went to a family gathering they would say things like **"You ruined your career."** or **"You could have been a star."** and I can't forget the all too famous line **"What Happened?"** Oh, and the ones that didn't say anything, their eyes spewed a million words the mouth couldn't speak. I felt like a failure. I wanted to die.

Months went by. I had a lot of alone time. Enough to know the stitching on my mother's couch by name. I'd sit there all day in the same position for hours. The remainder of my time was spent counting sheep and the number of rejected job applications in my email. Each day was a blur full of precipitation that wavered above my head to create a cloudy forecast of my future. Suddenly, there was a peak of sunshine. My phone vibrated. It felt like an earthquake. This would have been a completely regular occurrence if my battery without a doubt hadn't burned out a few hours before. I jumped out of bed to catch a glimpse of an angel. No luck. However, I did notice a number sequence that would shake my world. I picked up my phone. It read 3:33am, and the screen went blank.

I grew up on the end street of two religions. My father assembled in a mosque, and my mother went to church. I would visit my father on weekends until I grew out of it. A part of me resented him for leaving my mother. I will give credit to my father for providing me with somewhat of a spiritual foundation. He's a great teacher with a caring heart. Most of his teachings carried me through life.

Although I don't remember learning anything about numbers waking me up in the middle of the night. I wanted to know more. So I did what every millennial does when you want to time travel to the past, the present and the future. I turned to Google for answers.

To say I tiptoed around the caution sign of enlightenment is an understatement. I ran, slipped and fell down the rabbit hole of self-help. I consumed all of the information the Internet had readily available and picked up a few books from authors who don't get any credit on Instagram memes. The dots were starting to connect. Keywords like intuition, awareness, and plenty more you'll see throughout this book stood out to me. I needed a fresh start, and this world presented me with a new beginning. I stored the knowledge.

Numerology also started to resonate with me. Numbers like 11:11 and 555 appear daily. At first, I thought it was kind of weird, but the part of me that loves Harry Potter kept the magic alive.

The days started to drag. Even though I traveled far down the path of a spiritual awakening my current life was at a standstill. There was a slight shift in my spirit. I couldn't seem to astral travel, but I could go ghost on all my homies. My girlfriend at the time had another reason to think I was a complete lunatic. My mother could sense something was going on. We would have micro conversations that would always somehow end with her saying **"Nigga you ain't Jesus."** That's my mom. I stopped talking.

When I did speak, every word that came out of my mouth tied into self-development. I just didn't know how to apply any of that shit using practical sense. It was a cycle of ingesting and projecting. This is a preachy phase we all go through. If you're still in it, do yourself a favor and shut up. It's annoying.

A friend reached out. The kind of friend you can go months without hearing from. When you do, it's like you were with them yesterday. This time it was different. The distance was felt. My spirit went away on sabbatical and came back with insight. When we spoke, I couldn't articulate the inner change. We'll discuss more what to do when that happens in the next chapter. I settled for **"Yo bro."** He asked, **"How are you?"** I replied. "Somewhere in between losing my fucking mind and everything is going to be ok." We laughed as usual.

About a year before, we were rear-ended at a stoplight. Great for the bank account terrible for the back. My friend called to inform me the check had cleared on his end and to pick my brain on what to do with the cash. We did everything together. We were best friends and business partners. I spent most of my money on a music video we shot that never saw the light of day because of a hard-drive malfunction. This time around we wanted to use the settlement funds to do something worthwhile. It came down to two choices. Go to Vegas or move to Los Angeles.

Vegas peaked to the top of the list. We were excited to see a very popular female rapper hit the stage and gamble the night away. I had recently produced a song for the rapper's then-boyfriend. We thought it was all some sort of synchronicity where everything was aligning. While shuffling between options, every time moving to Los Angeles was mentioned a voice followed by a feeling of certainty would take over my body. This voice was nothing in comparison to my inner reading voice. It came to be direct, and bold yet not overpowering. Within seconds, I knew precisely what to do. I'd say I heard God. We know what my mother would say.

Waking The Dead

Kill Bill Volume 2 is definitely one of my favorite movies. There is a scene in the film where the lead actress has to claw her way through mounds of dirt to escape a casket before she suffocates. Classic. That's life. You have a choice to be present in the moment or die. Your friends, family, boss, and teachers will bury you alive beneath demands and expectations. You won't be able to breathe under pressure, and ultimately you will die a slow painful spiritual death. It's inevitable. I wish I'd known this before I got on the plane. Sometimes life gives us lemons we can't squeeze.

My decision to move to Los Angeles was a big lemon. In retrospect, my untimely demise could have been prevented if I didn't ignore the visible symptoms. Before we jump back into the story, let's check on the pulse of your spirit. Here are seven signs you may be spiritually dying.

1. You don't "feel" like it.
2. You're uncomfortable around old friends.
3. Ideas don't flow smoothly anymore.
4. You're somewhere between I'm stuck and "I'm growing."
5. Relationships are a struggle.
6. Everyone irritates the fuck out of you.
7. Life doesn't all the way suck, but it could be BETTER.

If you cringed through all of the above, I have some good news. You're a fully functional corpse! Pick your plot and prepare for a full reset and mental breakdown. Sounds fun right? Events will occur that will align you with your path and all that stuff your horoscope told you today. The bad news is you will be thrown in the most horrible situation and circumstances to force growth. Yup, it's time to pop that comfort bubble. Didn't think you'd be able to download the secrets of the universe without your battery dying once or twice right? C'mon you're smarter than that.

When I landed in LA, the red carpet was basically rolled out. My friend rented a beautiful downtown loft with cow print rugs spread across the marble floor. The security guards did their jobs, and I think the elevators talked back. I knew we couldn't afford it, but I had no control over the finances. I started looking for a job fast. The interviews were pouring in while the cash flow drained out. The adrenaline rushing through my glands wouldn't let the severity of the situation attack my drive. Every day was a race against the clock. Our overhead levitated over our bodies to see if we were still breathing. We were on life support.

LAX should have a sign that reads ***"Welcome to the city of angels. Gain a wing, destroy a soul."*** Don't get me wrong LA has its advantages. Networking, pretty girls, weed and don't get me started on Randy's Donuts. But my wings were sprouting fast. The airline ticket stub in my pocket reminded me I had no return date to fly home. The pressure was on. Things were getting serious.

When the term of our sublet expired, we grabbed our backpacks and boarded the next train to Hollywood. I remember gazing at the Hollywood sign. It's magnetic. Instantly you're sucked into a snapshot of all the dreams and desires of those who have laid eyes on it. Not such a great place to be amid a transition. You're completely vulnerable to all happenings. That same voice came to visit me. This time with the message **"You have to do this alone."** I was terrified. I ignored it and continued to look at the sign.

A thought is a seed from the tree of action. Almost immediately after receiving that message my mind started to shift. I kept thinking to myself maybe I can do this alone. My actions followed. I began building relationships with everyone from strangers on the street to the manager of the apartment complex we were renting. If you were to ask five people I encountered to describe my personality they'll probably give you five completely different answers. I'm more of an introvert, but I was functioning as an extrovert. It's like my body was on autopilot preparing for a zombie apocalypse. This could've been the early stages of schizophrenia or the traits of my Gemini sun, Virgo rising and Aquarius moon. I'll let you decide.

The day of reckoning came one sunny afternoon on the sunset strip. My friend met a girl. Ten minutes before the two of them met, I had given a full lecture on love, soulmates, and quantum physics so the events that took place after these words were entirely my fault. They hit it off and shortly after she moved in with us. Sounds strange? Not by Hollywood standards. I could write a novel on the weird stuff I've seen in Hollywood alone. I continued to drift. I would like to say we became a trio and busted some ghost, but that never happened. I became a ghost.

I found a job. I made sandwiches in thirty seconds for cash. Every day I'd walk three miles from a janky motel to catch the train for work. Three miles equates to one hour and twelve minutes of walk time. I didn't have a car and couldn't afford Uber. In between those seconds of the commute is where that inner voice would visit me.

Communication became an issue. My best friend and I didn't know each other anymore. Just people in passing. It was heartbreaking. I'll never forget the look on his face during our emotional fallout that led to a fistfight. The tension erupted as fast as I could put mayonnaise on a bun.

The streets are cold figuratively and literally. After the brawl, all ties were severed. I was officially homeless. Not fake homeless like when your mom kicks you out, and you stay with your grandma until it blows over. Real homeless like where the hell am I going to sleep tonight? I didn't panic. The voice affirmed things were under control. Were they? This was rock bottom.

Through silence and deep breathing within seconds, I remembered the relationship I built with the manager at an apartment complex. I reached out. The manager offered me two days in the basement of the building before anyone would find out he was hoarding humans. Two days was all I needed. On the first day, I found a second job at a club on Hollywood Blvd. On the last day, I talked him into giving me the passcode to get in the complex. That four-digit code was the key to my survival.

I had to find a way to protect myself. One duty of my job slinging subs was to deliver free product to the corporate offices downtown for leads. Instead, I handed out the sandwich samples across the park where the other homeless people slept. I'm sure they needed it more than the suits sitting behind a cubicle, plus I could get some rest without anyone bothering me. I now identified with this community. I knew how hard it was. Waking up on asphalt really grounds you. All actions count when your life is on the line. I snuggled in a corner behind a couple of bushes near the downtown public library. When I looked up, I could see the high-rise offices. I always wondered did anyone ever look out the window and see me sleeping.

I punched the clock on time every day. Why are you late again? I would use the four-digit code to sneak in the meter room of the apartment complex to get some secure rest. You never appreciate the walls until they're gone. I knew the exact usage of electricity for each unit. Before anyone could catch some creepy guy sleeping in the closet, I would be out of there by four in the morning and travel downtown to my fellow tenants of nature. I would repeat this same thing every day for weeks. My second job involved the night crowd. I was the guy standing on the corner giving you free admission tickets to get in the club before 11pm. The club let out is at 3am. I would stay out until 1am then walk to my closet, barely sleep and repeat. My body started to fail.

The lunchtime rush is dreadful. That's when I actually had to work. In the middle of perfecting my lettuce to meat ratio, my nose started gushing blood all over the condiments. I knew this wasn't good. I could count how many times I've experienced a nosebleed in my life. Someone's roast beef got a little extra sauce that day. My boss was kind enough to let me go home early. It's not like I needed the hours or a home for that matter. I appreciated the gesture. No one knew I was a street dweller. I played the role of a functional citizen very well.

I would wander for hours talking to people cycling through the apartment complex I fake rented. I used the leverage of people seeing my face every day to gain trust. If only they knew I had the power to shut off their lights.

The voice came to visit me one night in the meter room. This time, much louder. **"You're dying."** Not quite the message I was hoping for. It was true. My body felt weak. I contemplated on a makeshift noose from the clothes in my backpack to end it all. Before I could reach in my bag, I received another message. "Your lack of trust will kill you." Yoda is that you? Did someone slip a hallucinogen in my dinner? It felt surreal. The voice detached itself from my inner being. The presence filled the entire space. Until this point, I had almost lost my belief in any higher power. I say almost because the voice served as a pretty good guidance counselor however the circumstances were still pretty shitty. I knew I had to give myself over to this power to continue on. Suddenly my mouth spurted out two words that disrupted the frequency. **"I surrender."** This changed everything for me.

After I signed my deal with this source of energy it all turned around. It's like I had a cheat sheet to life. I landed my dream job working for a Grammy Award Winning engineer. I walked into meetings with major record labels on the same streets I slept on. I gained mentors that gave me priceless insight on business. I met a girl, I married the girl, and that girl had our beautiful baby girl. Not too bad for a guy who showered in a public restroom. My faith had been restored by my gratitude for life.

I'm no prophet or perfectionist. Maybe a bit of an idealist but who isn't. I still fail daily. It's a part of the process. The remaining chapters are about tapping in to the frequency of your inner voice to create an abundant lifestyle. God speaks through to us in the form of different mediums like concepts, principles, and keywords. Heaven exists to all who let go and be. Hell is created through resistance. You don't need to have a near death experience or be chosen to receive this power. It's ready for you right at this second.

The 20 Secrets Of Spiritual Wealth

The noise of the external world can be loud. With the voice of inner self completely submerged in life's distractions, it's no wonder you have anxiety, depression, and all the other self-sabotaging traits we humans have inherited. It's time to get quiet. It's time to listen. It's time to walk in your silence, or you'll never reach your full potential. You'll stay stuck in a rut. I died in that meter room. That inner voice, my higher self, God or whatever you see fit to call this source of power offered me the chance to live again and this time, I didn't decline the invite.

As promised, the remainder of this book is all yours. No fluff or words to fill the page to meet the publisher's quota. You're always one thought away from ruining your entire life. You don't need anymore clouding your judgment.

Ok, let's get to the shits.

listen.

Hear this often?

Make your next move your best move…

This statement is very vague and misleading.

I'm pretty sure if you knew your "next" move you would have made it yesterday.

There's a sweet spot in ignorance.

Take the apprehension and grab hold.

There is no right or wrong only concept.

What you don't understand today your spirit will tell you tomorrow.

The universe communicates through theory.

The mind processes through logic then the body reacts.

So, next time you're in the room with a firefighter don't talk about the fire.

Listen to how the flame was put out.

You'll know what to do next.

How to apply:

Find a quiet place. Spirit has to trust that you're listening to break through. Eliminate all distractions. No phone, no TV, no music. Just you and your higher self.

ideas.

Your ideas are love letters from your higher self.

This is single-handedly the most important romantic relationship you'll ever encounter throughout your journey.

Treat them as such.

Date your ideas.

Talk to them until the wee hours in the morning.

Take them out to fancy dinners and caress them into sleeping with you.

Let your mind and spirit have sex all night until you cum brilliant ideas.

Prove your commitment by procreating.

If it's not a fit, you'll know.

How to apply:

When you think of one write it down. Bad ideas count! Even if you think you'll remember it tomorrow chances are you won't. I jumped out of the shower to write this sentence.

ego.

Want to destroy your relationships?

Want to make life harder for yourself?

Want to block every opportunity the universe has made available?

Keep feeding your ego some jerk-o's for breakfast, and you WILL spiritually plateau.

Don't get me wrong. The ego has some deceitful advantages.

Your cute boyfriend

Your beautiful girlfriend

Your $400 sneakers

Peer admiration

All these things are worth value and validation.

However, don't make the mistake of attaching these things to your self-worth.

Here's why.

You're in a transition.

By the time you've made it through the full detachment of the ego, you'll feel completely empty.

The drive disappears.

You won't feel connected. You'll miss your "old" self.

Don't worry it's normal and you'll make it through.

I thought expressing my things and accolades on the outside would attract the friends and lifestyle I wanted.

Nope.

I used "things" and "people" to define who I was.

Don't be that guy.

How to apply:

Find people that are smarter and have accomplished more than you. Make them your friends. Don't let your insecurities make you feel inferior to them. Play the back, and peep game. You might learn something

empathize.

I didn't know how to feel.

I didn't empathize well with others.

I'd take things personally.

I was selfish.

I lived in my own world.

I had two choices.

I could blame everything and everyone for my shortcomings or

I could learn to feel.

Learn to feel daily.

Learn to understand.

Learn to see things from another perspective.

It's a muscle I work out daily.

Don't struggle with this.

People want to help you.

People want to communicate with you.

People love you.

Make yourself reachable.

Feel EVERYTHING.

How to apply:

Call someone right now. Say everything you'd typically say through text. Be receptive and at the end of the conversation express your appreciation for the recipient's point of view.

attachment.

Your personal attachment to winning may block you from receiving the energy of victory.

The act of detachment is key to building the momentum of success.

Let go of one thing today and start over tomorrow.

At one point I did ANYTHING to win. I was afraid to lose.

I only made a mess.

It's a scary feeling when you feel like it's all on the line.

Take some of the pressure off yourself today.

Maintain the balance between working and learning.

Protect your energy if you're not in the mood today.

Keep smiling.

How to apply:

Sell five items you absolutely love. This will not only clear up clutter around your home but also in your life. You'll learn to live a life free of any attachments.

comfort.

Find a new way to embarrass yourself every day.

This will build your comfort muscle.

If you're always afraid, you'll never ask.

If you're not smiling how can you attract your desires?

If you're not comfortable in your own skin, you'll never become your full authentic self.

How many opportunities are you passing up?

The projection of self-love will always leave an everlasting impression.

Mental note* to work at DISNEY you have to smile. I wonder why...

How to apply:

Try a new hairstyle. Date someone your family hates. Promote your selfies on social media. The more foolish you look in front of others the less you start to care about what they have to say.

balance.

Focus on the things or people that bring you peace.

Express the emotions that bring you closer to center.

Re-focus on the good in your life.

Everyone is busy. Life is in constant motion.

We're persistently juggling multiple hats on one head.

Accompany your daily demand with an anti-burnout regiment.

Find your happy medium.

Everyone is busy. Life demands so much from all of us.

How to apply:

Only talk to people you like. Gossip less. When you're sad cry it out. Don't bottle your emotions. Find ways to be creative. I believe everyone is an artist. Find your outlet.

persistence.

Everyone gives a good swing of the bat on the weekends.

By Monday the treats of that piñata of optimism turn into sour bites of depression.

Clean up all the self-sabotaging confetti on the floor of your mind.

Stay focus on your mission.

Appreciate another the full week to make purpose.

Your life is a party that never ends.

How to apply:

Fail often. Time stops moving when you stop trying. Apply the tactics you've acquired from one area in a different medium.

projection.

What do you want more of?

What's your discipline strategy?

Are you enjoying the process?

I wrote 50 songs a week sleeping in a dirty motel room.

This allowed me to attract meetings with publishers and record labels.

Not every song was a hit.

A few are really horrible actually.

The key is to create, release, repeat and not be attached to the outcome.

All it takes is ONE connection. Build that momentum.

Same rules apply for any profession.

Create. Release. Repeat.

This year you'll see the results you want.

How to apply:

Get into a routine. If you want to produce results you to be in rhythm with your higher self. Take 100 shots from the half court line one of those will be all net.

adapt.

While homeless, I meditated daily. When I went to work, no one knew I was living out of a backpack. I had more energy than some of my employees who hated their lives. This shifted my perspective.

Here are a few things I learned.

> Life happens in spurts.
>
> Take advantage of this period.
>
> Shake every hand. Soak up all game.
>
> No position is permanent.
>
> Where you are today, you won't be tomorrow.
>
> All happenings are connected.
>
> The universe works for you.
>
> The transition is in development.
>
> Be calm. Be still.

Use your environment.

At work, just sit in the restroom stall.

At home, go in the closet.

The answers are in front of you.

Every day counts.

How to apply:

Get out of your comfort zone. Move to a new city and make some lifelong memories. Your hometown is boring and depressing. I'm kidding, but if you're actually thinking about leaving, the next chapter is for you.

frequency.

Align with the energy of your goals.

Say, visualize, and feel the things you want.

Get specific.

Where do you live?

What are you driving?

What are you wearing?

How much money do you have?

Who are your friends?

Who are your mentors?

Pull it closer to you. Everything you need is available.

There is an unlimited amount of resources.

Shift your balance. Operate higher.

It's here now!

How to apply:

Pull your material needs closer to you through energy. You could rent a house you can't afford on Airbnb for a week or go to a car show to get behind the wheel of that new coupe. Do just about anything to surround yourself with the physical representation of your vision. Get some rich friends.

give.

No one is going to ask what YOU really want in life, what YOU love to do or who YOU really are on the inside.

YOUR job is to show up where it counts and GIVE more.

At times the people in our lives don't make it safe to reveal our REAL selves.

The things we like to do in our spare time or the ideas we think about but people will only know what you decide to show them.

Stop hiding from YOUR truth. If on the surface you're a painter and you actually love writing, write more. If on the surface you're a rapper but deep down you LOVE acting, go on more auditions! If you're at a 9-5 and want to freelance, create more. Give more to the world. Never stop the flow of your blessings because you're afraid of how it'll look on the outside or how others will perceive you. What you're currently doing may not be the thing you thought would leave your mark. Explore different versions of yourself to make the most impact while you're here. You're always ONE step closer to moving in your most authentic form.

We're multidimensional creatures of habit that long for a better understanding of one another.

If people don't understand or still trying to figure you out, don't say, "fuck em." GIVE more.

How to apply:

Give ideas to other people. Give your money away. Support your peer's endeavors. If you want more, you have to give more. Be grateful for your ability to communicate beyond physical reach.

optimism.

Explore the beauty of your mind.

Tomorrow is the enemy of creativity.

Write that goal.

Sketch that drawing.

Note that joke. Voice memo that song.

An idea is a paintbrush to the blank canvas of life.

If you're feeling blue, add some color to the world.

No thought has boundaries.

Today is your day. Create.

How to apply:

Serotonin is the happy hormone. Every time you get a like on your Instagram picture that chemical is released. If you average six double taps like me, you're probably about to jump off a cliff. Don't worry just eat serotonin rich foods like bananas or snack on some nuts. Listening to your favorite music also helps. Not everyone can be an influencer. Please follow me @adecruse thanks in advance.

surrender.

Does it feel like you've tried everything?

You're on GO. Always thinking of the next.

I understand. Try this.

Find a safe and quiet place. Prep your body.

Allow the messages to come through.

What's the next step?

Surrender your power to the source.

The images will come to your mind. The answers will be revealed.

Don't create unnecessary work for yourself.

There's an internal compass implanted in each of us.

You already know all that you know. Let it flow.

How to apply:

Ok, this is probably the hardest to implement. Trust that all will be revealed when operating from within. I know, listening to some unknown source of power doesn't serve you well in real life. Energy can't pay the bills, right? Wrong, your ability to listen for answers and surrender to the process will open a new route and pave the road to endless opportunities. Remember, the universe is limitless.

action.

Contemplating on a decision?

Take the leap. Don't worry about the details.

Put yourself in a position to be afraid and uncertain.

Not only will you uncover new details about yourself you'll

a) Force growth.

b) Have a better understanding of what you like, love and hate.

c) Learn to rely less on your conscious mind.

d) Free up any stagnant energy you may unknowingly carry.

Motion is key. Get moving.

Things are a lot scarier in our heads.

Trust that your higher self will reveal the next steps when needed.

You're being guided.

Hesitation is the enemy of progress.

Stop getting in your own way.

Positive changes are coming for you.

Jump into it!

How to apply:

If you're thinking about doing it, just do it. Even if it's life-threatening, you could use the lesson.

intention.

Get your thoughts out and put it on paper.

Your subconscious has to be reminded of what you desire consistently.

Make it scalable.

You're not going to own a house, travel the world and make 1 million dollars in one day.

However, the signal you send to the universe is multiplied within seconds.

Let your vision maturate.

I find it easier to direct your focus on 5 - 7 intentions throughout six to twelve months.

After work, school or whatever you have going on.

Go to your nearest dollar store and get some supplies.

All you need is poster board, a magazine, and your vision.

If you're setting a financial intention:

I'd use images from a magazine like Vogue to draw in higher frequencies.

Cut out images that represent what you see in your head.

Share it with your friends.

Find an accountability partner!

Check in with them every month to see where both of you are with your goals.

Stick it somewhere you're forced to see it every day.

Suggestions:

Front, bedroom or bathroom door.

How to apply:

I curated content by microblogging in 60 days and used most of that material to write this book. Start small. Set obtainable goals. Everyone wants to build Rome in a day. If you have a goal to make $10,000, think of ten ways to make $1000. Don't burn yourself out shooting for that million-dollar thought.

fear.

Your purpose is more significant than what you can see in front of you.

Fear will trick you into believing you don't have any potential.

Anxiety will make you feel like you're against the clock of your own time.

Your conscious mind will only process the nature of the physical world.

Don't let your personal inadequacy deter you from the goal.

All thoughts matter good and bad.

Don't beat yourself up.

You belong here.

Life is a high. If you overthink, you'll have a bad trip.

Tap in.

How to apply:

Activate your instincts. Put yourself in a situation where your higher self has to come through.

gratitude.

When your old life doesn't fit, take it back to the universe.

Show your gratitude receipt and exchange it for enlightenment.

Step into your element.

Stop settling for half of yourself.

Let's say you make the best spaghetti sauce and everyone knows it.

Every bone in your body quakes when you think about making a living selling your recipe.

Instead of acting on it, you decide to ignore those feelings because of whatever excuse you make up at the moment.

Guess what?

You just gave the middle finger to the universe.

The universe is keeping note and next time around you'll get skipped when it's handing out orders.

That's how this works.

Stop being picky.

Take what's given.

If God invites you over for dinner, you better eat.

How to apply:

Before you go to sleep, think of five people you're grateful for. Kill them in the next thought. If they all died how would you operate? Treat them with the same emotion of the last sentence. Appreciate the cognitive process.

growth.

Your body is housing the spirit.

Don't halt the process of development.

Embody the art of remodeling.

Fight for your new self.

The person you're most afraid to talk to will become your best friend.

The food you never thought you'd try will become your favorite recipe.

The idea you never executed is the one that will have the most impact.

Fear not the ability to magnify but the incapacity to recognize your real potential.

Like a beetle, we too have an exoskeleton.

Shed daily.

How to apply:

Stay in the cut until you're ready to play. Let your friends and family know you're going through some internal changes. I guarantee they will appreciate the honesty and give you space. Going MIA completely makes you look crazy. Communication is everything.

forgiveness.

The recurring patterns of trauma can end with us. When I was 12, my mother called me in her room after dinner, pinned me against the wall and threatened to commit suicide. The nozzle of a 40-caliber pistol against the temple of your care provider is not a pretty sight. I internalized the fear and carried it with me for years. It wasn't until I shifted my perspective to realize how much of a beautiful experience it was even to have gone through it in the first place.

Raising two kids as a single parent is no easy feat. It didn't help that my little brother and I were behaving as descendants of Satan. Sorry, mom, I understand now. That pain I lugged around gave me the power to detach myself from the fear of the outside world. I didn't care what other people thought of me because I already felt betrayed. Betrayed by my father for not being there and by my mother for her lack of judgment.

Trauma is a gift of the divine. All that pain you're withholding is causing a vibration blockage. Maybe you're the child of a single parent. Perhaps you have a drug problem or suffering from a tragic loss of a loved one. Whatever it is, embrace it! Send that signal to the source. The higher self is trying to communicate with you regularly. It can't break through if you are resisting. Give it to the universe in exchange for supernatural abilities. Your pain is a superpower. It's a beautiful part of you. It's not meant to eat away at your core. Express it proactively. Translate the same emotion you put into being angry and filter it through constructive activity. Add value to others that have gone through similar happenings and those closed off experiences will start to shift.

How to apply:

Parents.

Forgive yourself.

Although it's your job to protect your child, blind spots can occur at any moment. It's not your fault. Stop holding guilt over the trauma you had no control over. It doesn't make you a bad parent if you made a mistake. When your child is suffering, continue to provide support the best way you know how and express your love language regularly.

Kids.

Forgive your parents.

They're doing the best they can. We're all struggling to make the best decisions we can with the options available.

Never make them feel uncomfortable in any way. When your child is hurting, it's not a good feeling to internalize. Be aware of the energy you're projecting towards them. Passive aggressive behavior is a sign of resentment.

*Keep in mind

They've already been through it OVER and OVER again in their mind of how and why you're hurting. Show your appreciation. Empathize and understand the generation gap.

The communication is different. The struggle is different. If you're going to make a difference in the world for the sake of the future generation, let it go.

__What happened is done. Place blame on none.__

"Rule Of P."

The rule of thirds is something you learn in photography class about balance and composition. I went to art school where they teach you to break the rules. I actually wanted to finish the book with no conclusion, but every English teacher who has believed in my writing would kill me. With that in mind, I'll leave you with three principles of life with words that start with the letter P.

Purpose.

The universe doesn't pick favorites.

Make yourself available to receive all that it has to give.

Chaos is the prelude to miracles.

If your life isn't in shambles, you're playing it too safe.

Terrible things have to happen to bring out the greatness within.

The possibilities of life are limitless.

Belief and faith are the parents to personal fulfillment.

Don't be a brat.

Progress.

A little bit goes a long way.

Work on a small percentage of your goal every day.

Don't overdo it.

You won't hit it out the park every swing.

Step away from the plate to see what's happening on the field.

Welcome failure with a hug and kiss.

BIG ideas manifest themselves in small increments.

Frustration is normal.

Be kind to yourself.

Mastery doesn't happen overnight.

Patience.

In the digital age of information, everybody is everything.

I've read articles about social media being linked to anxiety and depression.

I'd say I'm 50/50 on that argument.

If anything, technology aids in the process of self-discovery.

Stop brushing off your feelings.

You KNOW what you're here to do.

If you don't know, use social media to align with people you want to be like.

Frequency travels.

See your vision through from beginning to the end.

Time will provide answers. Take in your experience.

Appreciate your journey.

Where you are is where you belong.

Take account of what you ask the universe for and don't freak out when it doesn't happen right away.

There's just enough space in the sky for your star to shine brightly.

Keep shinning.

Leap of Faith Index

I ran away from home once as a kid. For about twenty minutes I walked around my neighborhood searching for a family to take me in. I rang the bell of a senior woman who immediately slammed the door in my face after I presented my offer. Within an hour I was back home because it started to snow. I felt rejected. This experience contributed to my fearlessness. Stepping out on faith can be terrifying. There is no guide to jumping. You just have to jump, fly and like Woody told Buzz in the movie Toy Story "Fall with style." So, on your way down here are some gliding techniques to apply.

A

Ask for help

Answer your phone calls and emails.

Allow yourself to be hurt.

B

Be yourself.

Be aware.

Bounce around ideas.

C

Call home they miss you.

Concrete is surprisingly good for the back.

Concentrate on the objective.

D

Don't get caught slippin'.

Drink water.

Despite the circumstances, you're still alive.

E

Enjoy the process.

Everyone is your friend. (You don't have time for enemies.)

Evaluate your options.

F

Fuck your pride.

Focus on your breath.

Find your tribe.

G

Go today not tomorrow.

Guidance is available to those who seek.

Get acclimated to your environment.

H

Healthy alternatives can be found at 7-Eleven.

Homesick? Don't look back.

Heroin highs can last for 8 hours. Use your time wisely.

I

Initiate the conversation.

Invest in yourself.

Ignore the critics.

J

Jump without hesitation.

Jealousy is the gateway drug to introspection.

Join the club of dreamers once before you.

K

Kill fear.

Kind words and a smile will get people to trust you.

Know that you know.

L

Let go.

Lose the attitude.

Live in the moment.

M

Money can't buy you good energy.

Mindfulness is next to godliness.

Make mistakes.

N

Never look back.

Nature resets the soul.

No pain no gain.

O

Operate from within.

Only go outside to do things you like.

Overproduce. Over deliver.

P

Push through the negative emotions.

Promote yourself.

Pack light. (Like really light.)

Q

Quit ya bitchin'.

Quiet the mind.

Quick decisions are usually the best.

R

Rest when necessary.

Real recognize real.

Reality is what you make it.

S

Stop overthinking.

Surrender to the source.

Sublets are suitable for passing the time.

T

Take care of your health. Free clinics are everywhere.

Time is linear.

The voice of your higher self is always present.

U

Universal law is working for you.

Understanding is a pursuit, not the destination.

Unlearn all that you know.

V

Validity is rewarded through service.

Visualize the next steps.

Vacuum self-sabotaging thoughts. (They're dirty)

W

With all you know. What will you do?

War of the mind is fatal to the spirit.

Winters suck. Move to a warmer place.

X

Xylophones are fun to play.

Xanax helps when driving across the country.

Xmas is coming. Buy this book for a friend.

Y

You are in control.

Yelling makes things worse.

Yoga helps.

Z

Zelle is way faster than Western Union.

Ziploc bags come in handy.

Zombies are people afraid to live.

Ade Cruse is a music producer, film composer, and writer with aspirations of owning a pet pig. Spare time activities include hiking, watching the sunset, and consuming an unhealthy amount of strawberry or vanilla milkshakes.

cruseART Publishing

Want more spiritual goodies? Visit cruseART.shop for the latest.

www.ingramcontent.com/pod-product-compliance
Lightning Source LLC
Chambersburg PA
CBHW021958290426
44108CB00012B/1126